Delayed Gratification

12 Principles for Achieving Financial Freedom

Congratulations! Someone cares about you and wants you to have your own copy.

To: _____

From: _____

Pass it on!

Delayed Gratification

12 Principles for Achieving Financial Freedom

By **Rick Katz**

Contributions by

Kyle Counts

Jeff Benne

Carletha Rogers

Published by Richard H. Katz
© 2014

©Entire Contents Copyrighted, 2007-2014, Richard H. Katz

All Rights Reserved. **BUT**, if you would like to help others by sharing this information, please contact me so I can grant you permission to share.

Now that that's out of the way, open your mind and consider a better way to get a better result. Enjoy the book and tell your friends and family. Become an advocate of great results through Delayed Gratification and Planning Ahead.

As Jeremy said,

"A Children's Book for Grown Ups"

First Printing: 8/2014
Second Printing: 10/2014
ISBN: 9781500821302

www.RickKatz.com

"People who plan ahead have better results and live more enjoyable lives than those who wing it; wouldn't you agree?."

Rick Katz

Dedication

This book is dedicated to some outstanding women in my life. Guys, take heed. We know that financial freedom cannot be achieved without the collaboration, watchful eye and diligence of the women in our lives.

To my **Wife**, Carlyn Katz, who is beautiful, brilliant, engaging, loving and romantic. She truly brings out the best in me and everyone in her life. You are my inspiration to be the best version of me. I love you.

To my **Sister**, Linda Grife, who is bright, inspirational, motivating and the most optimistic person I know. She has three brothers (including me) who aspired to find a woman just like her to marry. May your battle with cancer be brief and completely successful.

To my **Daughter**, Ashley Katz, who is intelligent, a natural leader, beautiful, ambitious, adventurous and creative. Her success and enthusiasm are contagious to all those around her. Live the life you have imagined, Ashee. You're awesome!

Table of Contents

		Page
Introduction	An underlying Principle	3
Principle 1	The numbers reveal reality	7
Principle 2	Attitude is a choice	13
Principle 3	Avoid failure	21
Principle 4	You have the power	31
Principle 5	Nothing changes without action	35
Principle 6	Heed the wisdom of the wise	45
Principle 7	Don't do it alone	55
Principle 8	Occam's Razor	67
Principle 9	Know where you are	75
Principle 10	Have a plan	83
Principle 11	Baby steps	91
Principle 12	Overcome the fear	103
Conclusion	Bring it all home	107
Index of Quotes		117

"If you want something above average, you have to do something the average are not willing to do."

Rick Katz

Forward

I've known Rick Katz for over 13 years now. What started out as a client relationship became a venture partnership and has developed into a lifelong friendship. I've followed Rick's career over the years and what has always stood out and remains constant are his integrity, his intelligence, and his philosophies.

This book is a reflection of who Rick is as a person. In it, he shares the philosophies that have made him successful and have helped him make a difference in the lives of those around him. Although the book is focused on offering practical guidance about how to achieve financial freedom, the lessons apply to success in general and can help anyone improve any part of their life.

Rick's book is an easy read. His ideas are easy to understand and he makes them easy to implement. Use his wisdom to make a difference in your life. Achieve financial success. Make smarter decisions. Have better focus. And lead a happier, more satisfying life.

Michael Beck
Executive Strategist
Michael Beck International   www.MichaelJBeck.com

_____

_____

"Go confidently into the directions of your dreams. Live the life you have imagined"

Henry David Thoreau

Preface

My goal is to help you achieve economic independence and financial security by following proven, successful principles and ideas for acquiring money and other assets and keeping the assets. This book will guide you through simple, step-by-step principles for financial self-discipline. They are designed to help you develop the wealth-building habits, including short-term spending plans, long-term preparation, life insurance planning and retirement preparation that best meet your individual needs. You will be better equipped to creatively and quickly resolve any present financial problems and prevent future ones from arising.

You have to Create Intentional Success. Create means doing something differently to get a better result. Intentional assures that it is all about predictability and within your control. Success must be measurable so you know when you arrive. You must practice delayed gratification and have confidence in the outcome.

It is my hope that this book will put you on the road to financial security and freedom by providing perspective and tools to accomplish this. As you travel along this road, stay focused on your goals. They will keep you going in the right direction and will help you make positive and responsible spending decisions.

Caution: The ideas in this book may lead to considerable lifestyle changes. You will now answer the phone when it rings, no longer afraid that it may be a creditor. So-called financial emergencies, such as buying tires, will seem like inconveniences, not catastrophes. Financial opportunities may present themselves in places you've never seen before and you will be in a position to take advantage of them. Work hard, stay focused, and share your dreams and goals with others.

Rick

"Some average men use the words of great men so others may think they are great themselves."

John Adams

In addition to the 12 Principles for Achieving Financial Freedom, there are also

12 Major Goals and Obstacles

in one's life that must be considered. Some may not be relevant and most will be significant. You must consider *if* the Goal/Obstacle is important and *when* it will be most important. Throughout the book, I will illustrate and explain each of these life events beginning with this one.

Survivor Needs

The most financially catastrophic event that can happen in your family's life is your death. Is it important to you that your family is protected from this event? When will it begin being significant?

An Underlying Principle

The Marshmallow Test

The Marshmallow Test

*"The **Marshmallow Experiment**" was a series of studies on delayed gratification in the late 1960s and early 1970s led by psychologist Walter Mischel, then a professor at Stanford University. In these studies, a child was offered a choice between one small reward (commonly a marshmallow) provided immediately or two small rewards if he or she waited until the tester returned (after an absence of approximately 15 minutes).*

In the initial and follow-up studies, the researchers found that children who were able to wait longer for the preferred rewards tended to <u>have better life outcomes</u>, as measured by SAT scores, educational attainment, body mass index (BMI) and other life measures.

A 2011 brain imaging study of a sample from the original Stanford participants when they reached mid-life showed key differences between those with high delay times and those with low delay times in two areas: the prefrontal cortex (more active in high delayers) and the ventral striatum (an area linked to addictions) when they were trying to control their responses to alluring temptations.[1]

Science shows us that delayed gratification and reliability in the outcome creates more favorable results than those impatient and seeking the here and now. This can be a learned behavior. In order for the delayed gratification to pay off, one must have confidence in the ultimate outcome. This is not as difficult as one may imagine.

PLAY AT HOME VERSION: This is an interesting project to attempt on children from the ages of about 3 to 8 years old. Create your own experiment to see if your child has already acquired the value of delayed gratification versus immediate gratification. Offer the child a marshmallow now - or 3 marshmallows if they wait and do not eat the marshmallow immediately. Ask that they wait 10 full minutes for the richer reward. There is no negative outcome; rather, this may serve as a guide for how much effort should be put forth teaching the concept and habit.

After all, people who take the time to plan ahead will have more successful and enjoyable lives than those that wing it; don't you agree?

[1] Wikipedia, the free encyclopedia, "Stanford marshmallow experiment"

"It is never too late to become what you might have been"

George Eliot

Principle 1

The numbers reveal reality

The 100 Person Story

It is important that you know what the numbers reveal and what your true opportunity is over time. So, what are the results? If we took a typical group of 25 year old individuals and followed them throughout their lives until age 65, this is what we would find:

29   Have passed away

63   Are Dependent on others

3   Are still working

5   Are financially independent

But, only **1** person out of 100 would be considered financially well off, having the choices and flexibility to live as they want. In which group would you like to find yourself? While you do not have control over all of these outcomes, you most likely have more control than you think. Take control of that which you can. Continue to ask yourself, "What if…"

People who plan ahead have better results and live more enjoyable lives than those who wing it. It took your entire life to build your current circumstances. It is not reasonable to think you can fix it by Tuesday. But, you can **start** on Tuesday. The time to begin planning ahead is now.

This may be a difficult conversation to have, but it is critical that you face reality to create a new reality. Don't feel like you are the only person that has not saved as you should have or used credit cards too much. The company you keep is challenged with these same issues. **The main thing is to keep the main thing, the main thing.**

Family Care-giving

At some point in your life, do you believe it may become necessary for you to care for a loved-one? Later on in your life, will one of your children have to take care of you? Planning ahead can reduce the emotional, logistical and financial impact of family care-giving. Is it important to you that your family is protected from this event? When will it begin being significant?

"If you always do what you have always done, you will always get what you have always gotten. Therefore, to get something you have never had, you have to do something you've never done."

Rick Katz

Retirement Preparation

At some point in the future, you may want to retire. That will require you to amass assets that can be converted into income. Is it important to you to begin planning and savings in anticipation of retirement? When will it begin being significant?

Principle 2

Attitude is a choice

It's all about Attitude

Every morning when we wake up, we are faced by important decisions. Perhaps the most important decision we can make is whether to have a positive or negative attitude.

This may come as a surprise to you. Most people don't think of their attitude as something they have any control over. They think that attitude is determined by external circumstances, or that they're essentially positive or negative in nature or that they vacillate between the two extremes. But the truth is that your attitude is largely something you can choose. I will help you learn how to change your habitual ways of thinking to develop a more positive attitude.

Attitude is the mirror of the heart and mind. It can be understood as a manner of acting, feeling or thinking that reveals a person's disposition, such as sympathetic, friendly, unfriendly or hostile. The decision we make about our attitude determines what kind of day we are going to have, or perhaps more correctly, what kind of day we are going to *make for ourselves*. Our attitude affects others as well - families, friends, and co-workers.

A good attitude for us to adopt is the "can do" attitude, which is optimistic in nature. Positive thinking of this sort leads to positive decisions, which usually lead to positive results. Conversely, negative thinking generally leads to negative decisions and, thus, negative outcomes.

Countless stories are told of military service members being held captive by foreign powers for extended periods of time with only their training and attitudes available to allow them to overcome challenges of will, courage, and survival. By remaining focused on the task at hand, one's resolve can accomplish outstanding achievements.

A positive attitude about money and our day-to-day spending habits helps us better handle our financial resources. A part of this involves keeping wealth and money in the proper perspective. They say that money cannot buy happiness, which is true; but, it can give you the freedom to live the life you have imagined and give you the strength to help others. Sounds worth it to me.

Webster's New World Dictionary defines **wealth** as:

(1)(a) Much money or prosperity; great amount of worldly possessions.
  (b) The state of having much money or property; affluence.
(2) A large amount (of something); abundance (a wealth of ideas).
(3) Valuable products, contents or derivatives (the wealth of the oceans).
(4) Well-being.
(5)(a) Everything having economic value measurable in price.
  (b) Any useful material capable of being bought, sold, or stocked for future disposition.

Usually we think of wealth as consisting of money or possessions. But a rich reward doesn't necessarily mean lots of money. It can also mean having the freedom and well-being to find success in *every* aspect of life. This is the positive outlook.

Does your way of thinking about money need adjustment or changing? If you really wish to make changes in your attitude, you must be willing to assess your current opinions, values, practices, and patterns. An easy, if sometimes uncomfortable, way to find out if you are a positive or negative person is to seek feedback from your family, friends, and colleagues on how they view your attitude. You may get an earful but, if you can stay objective and put their responses in perspective, the feedback can help you make changes toward a new and exciting way of life.

Ask yourself the following questions:

1. Am I more likely to focus on problems rather than solutions?

2. Do I regularly verbalize optimism?

3. Is it my nature to seek alternatives before making decisions?

4. Are there several optimistic, positive thinking people in my life who may influence my thinking and disposition?

5. Can I point to specific circumstances in which positive thinking and creative approaches helped

transform a negative situation into a positive one?

Once we understand our own frame of mind, we can begin to implement practical, daily changes. Day by day you will begin to shed the old ways of doing things—the old habits, the old sayings, and the old (perhaps impulsive) ways of making decisions. They will be replaced by new ideas, constructive habits, and sound decision-making methods.

"I have not failed. I've just found 10,000 ways that won't work."

Thomas Edison

Birth of A Child

Are you planning ion having children? If you are beyond that, do you have a desire to "support" or "help out" with grandchildren or someone else's children? When will it begin being important?

Principle 3

Avoid failure

Why do people fail?

By first looking to why people fail, we may gain insights into how one can succeed. These barriers to success are easy to overcome, but only when you know they're there. Why do some people achieve their goals while others fail? It may be because successful people manage to overcome common barriers that, in many cases, guarantee failure.

Here are the 5 Reasons People Fail & What to Do Instead:

1. Uninspiring Goals

When most people set goals, they envision a thing (such as a particular amount of money), an object (like a new car), or a specific achievement (like writing a book). Unfortunately, these "things I'm going to get or do" goals don't appeal to the core of what motivates you, because they miss the point that what you're actually seeking in life and work is the POSITIVE EMOTIONS that you believe those things will produce.

Fix: Rather than envisioning a thing as your goal, envision--with all the strength in your imagination--how you will *feel* when you achieve the goal. That way, you'll be inspired to do whatever it takes (within legal and ethical bounds) to achieve that goal.

2. Fear of Failure

If you are afraid of failing, you won't take the necessary risks required to achieve your goal. For example, you won't make that important phone call because you're afraid that you'll be rebuffed. Or, you won't quit your dead-end job and start your own business because you're afraid that you might end up without any money.

Fix: Decide--right now!--that failure, for you, is a strictly temporary condition. If things don't go the way you'd like, it's only a setback that, at most, delays your eventual success. In other words, accept the fact that you'll sometimes fail, but treat that failure as an unavoidable - yet vital - component in your quest.

3. Fear of Success

In many ways, this fear is even more debilitating than the fear of failure. Suppose you achieved something spectacular, such as enormous wealth. What if it didn't make you happy? What then? What if you ended up losing all of it? What then? Would your friends start acting weird? Would your family be envious? Such thoughts, and they are common, can cause even a highly motivated person to self-sabotage.

Fix: Decide that you're going to be happy and grateful today and happy and grateful in the future, no matter what happens. Rather than focus on possible problems, envision how wonderful it would be to be able to help your friends and family achieve THEIR goals.

4. An Unrealistic Timetable

Most people vastly overestimate what they can do in a week and vastly underestimate what they can do in a year. Because of this, most people try to cram too many action items into the short term rather than spacing out activities over the long term. The inability to get all the short-term steps accomplished creates discouragement and the impression that the final goal is slipping away.

Fix: As you list the activities and steps required to achieve a goal, schedule only the 20% of the activities that will produce 80% of your results. Beyond that, set ambitious long-term timetables, but always leave some wiggle room when you plan short term.

5. Worrying About Dry Spells

It's easy to get discouraged when you reach a point at which nothing you do seems to advance you toward your goal. For example, suppose you're trying to master a certain skill. You make swift progress at first but then, after a while, it seems as if you're not doing any better, or maybe a little worse. Some people use these plateaus or dry spells as an excuse to give up and, therefore, fail.

Fix: Whenever you reach a plateau or dry spell, it's time to celebrate rather than give up. A plateau is almost always a sign that you're on the brink of a major breakthrough *if* you just have the patience to stick with it and trust that you'll eventually achieve your goal.

"People say that money is not the key to happiness, but I always figured if you have enough money, you can have a key made.

Joan Rivers

Are you open to new success ideas? Attitudes are the mirror of the mind. They guide our thoughts, conversations, and decisions. It's our daily successes and failures that mold and shape our values, attitudes, and decisions. Our immediate reactions to these daily events––what we learn from them and what we do about improving the future—is what makes us who and what we are as a person. Is your attitude toward the future one of positive anticipation or fearful apprehension?

How has your financial life been going? If things have been great (that is, you are blessed and financially you have saved, invested, and reached your stated goals) then pat yourself on the back and keep on going. Barring something catastrophic, it is more than likely that the next few years will mirror those that came before and few changes will be necessary. To put it another way, as long as you have more wins than losses, you should keep playing the game.

On the other hand, if blessings seem to be few, there are lots of distractions, your savings are minimal, and investments are still on the things-to-do list, then chances are the next few years will not be very different—unless you make some changes now.

When does change begin? *With the willingness to consider change.* Remember, our thoughts go where we send them. Consider the many advantages of sending our minds toward positive, productive thoughts instead of unproductive, negative thinking and worry. The all-important attitude decision sets the tone for the entire day. It means the difference between being receptive or closed-minded, harmony or contention, creative thinking or worry.

It is our attitudes, backed by fortitude, that will propel us farther along in every aspect of our lives - not simply our aptitudes. People typically succeed or fail because of their attitude and behaviors, not because of their intelligence or lack of knowledge.

We need to practice looking for possibilities and opportunities. Send your mind to higher and higher thoughts, greater and greater possibilities. Begin today thinking ever more positive, prosperous thoughts. Become a more thoughtful person, one full of positive and creative thoughts.

At this point you may be thinking, "Sounds great, but

what am I supposed to *do?" Start by expecting to be successful.* The following exercise will help you build a track record of financial responsibility and will provide you with the confidence to approach your finances with optimism and a positive attitude. How strong are you…really?

Mortgage Needs

This goal may be any of the following:

1. You are renting and desire to buy a home.

2. You own a home and want to refinance to lower your rate and payment.

3. You aspire to own rental property.

Are any of these aspirations of yours? When will it begin being significant?

Principle 4

You have the power

The 80% Solution

There is so much in our lives that we cannot control. We cannot affect the stock market, actions of others, many obstacles and more. Therefore, it is essential that we seize responsibility of that which we can control. While this idea might sound oversimplified, its power is unquestionable. Here is an idea that will keep you financially fit throughout your life, regardless of your income level. Imagine having the money you need when you need it. Imagine never struggling to pay your bills or other unexpected expenses. Imagine retiring on time and with all the assets you planned on having.

While this idea sounds like a title to a book, it is such a simple, yet effective concept, that I will share it with you on just a couple of pages. Here's how it works. Whatever your income is at any given point in your life, just take 80% of that amount to create a budget. The other 20% is dedicated to your future. It is taken off the top before you spend a dollar on your budget. For example, if you earned $60,000 a year ($5,000/month), your take-home pay would be about $3,650 after taxes and benefits. Take $720/month and invest into your future (20%) and then create a budget for $2,920 of income. It is crucial that you create the discipline to take the 20% off the top and then spend on your current lifestyle.

About 97% of people spend their money first (without a budget) and save what's left over, if there is any left over. That means only 3% save first and spend what's left over. Pay yourself first! Why wouldn't you invest in yourself first by putting away something for the future? People who plan ahead have better results and live more enjoyable lives that those who wing it. It all starts with your attitude. Just decide to do it.

You may be thinking that you cannot cut your spending to 80% of your income now. That's fine. Just look to the future and every time you get a raise or promotion, dedicate a portion of your increase in compensation to this concept and in a few years you will have grown into an 80% solution. Just pay yourself first!

By the way, the 70% Solution will actually result in greater wealth. Grow into 80% over a period of time and then grow into 70%. Then, live the life you have imagined.

"Wealth is the ability to fully experience life."

Henry David Thoreau

Principle 5

Nothing changes without action

Exercise: The Thirty-Day Savings Plan through *Change* Management

Try this simple exercise for the next thirty days. If you are successful, you will have the confidence to move on to the bigger financial challenges — and you will have earned an extra $20-$40. This plan does not require you to make any adjustments in your current spending habits. Keep buying what you normally buy. But here's the difference:

*First, carry cash and stop using your debit or credit card. Each time you make a **cash** purchase, always give the cashier bills without any coins. Even resist the temptation to provide the two pennies for a $6.02 purchase.*

Next, take all of those loose coins (you receive as change) out of your pocket every day for this 30 day period. Put all the money in a jar. Do not spend any of it. If you stick to this simple two-step plan, you will have put away an average of fifty cents on every purchase you make for the next month. The average consumer makes between forty and eighty transactions a month. Although this may sound like a lot of purchases, it's not when you consider how often you buy a candy bar, a coffee, newspaper, etc. The money you put aside by following this plan will pay for this book many times over and will put you in a position of thinking about other ways you can replace poor spending and savings habits with better ones.

Adjusting your attitude toward spending will help you change your money habits so they won't be changed for you. Making these changes will not be nearly as fun or rewarding if they are forced upon you by a lack of money.

Imagine $30 extra per month without changing your buying or spending habits!

The most important lesson to be learned is...

Change before you have to change.

Here are some additional steps that will help you get into the habit of changing your habitual behaviors. Some examples of things to work on might be eliminating smoking, controlling or reducing weight, earning certifications or promotions, or just being positive and listening before answering. It's always best to *initiate action yourself* instead of waiting for external circumstances to force you to make changes.

1. Write down what it is you want to do and why.
   Keep it simple at first and be specific.

2. Look for daily applications.
   Think about it each time you pull out your wallet.

3. Be regular and diligent in your effort.
   Stick to the plan and reap the rewards.

4. Talk about it with one or two trusted friends, a family member or superiors.

Don't underestimate the value of experiences from those who came before you.

5. Say it aloud to yourself several times each day.
   It won't sound as foreign or seem as hard if it sounds familiar.

6. Place visual reminders all over your home, office, work space or car.
   Hang up a picture of your goal so that you see it several times each day.

7. Go to a class or get books and articles to read that will create awareness.
   "If money is your hope for independence you will never have it. The only real security that a man will have in this world is a reserve of knowledge, experience, and ability." Henry Ford

8. Visualize yourself in the newly modified mode.
   Picture what you might look like and feel like if all your bills were paid and you had $25,000 in the bank.

College Expenses

Do you want to go to college or do you want to assist your children to go to college. Are you aware of the cost? Perhaps you can share the cost with your children. After all, an education can be financed but retirement cannot. Planning ahead will make achieving this goal easier. When will it begin being significant?

"The glow of one warm thought is to me worth more than money."

Thomas Jefferson

Knowledge, Attitudes, and Habits

There are three basic things in life we can change. We can increase our knowledge by learning new things, which is relatively easy for most people. We can change our attitudes, which is a bit more difficult. And lastly, we can change our habits. Changing habits doesn't occur in an afternoon, overnight, or even in a week.

Why? Because habits took longer than that to develop, which means they will most likely require more than a casual approach to modify, improve, or change them completely. Notice there is no reference made to "breaking" a habit, since people don't do that too well. Trying to stop something often creates a vacuum and unless replaced by something of a positive nature, eventually the vacuum will burst and people often find themselves right back into the old habits.

Keep in mind that *changing* or *modifying* a habit is easier than *breaking* one too. You don't want to find yourself slipping back into those old habits again. *Modifying* a habit works better because your mind is focusing on a new area of interest and not always on the negative of not doing something habitually. Feeding and filling your mind with wonderful ways to do new things in your life will soon, with self-discipline, crowd the old habits into the background and, eventually, out of existence.

A major reason why habits stay habits is that they never become an area of focus in our minds until there is intervention. Then, change is either mandated by external conditions such as health, marital discord, problems on the job, or financial difficulties. Rarely is it motivated by internal decisions to bring about positive changes in our lives before trouble starts.

We can make a complete and absolute change in habits, thinking and attitudes over time with determination. Be patient. Most of our habits and values were formulated over an extended period of time. Guiding principles make it easier to stay focused on the desired behavior.

Sometimes, these principles can be best related by professionals. Let's take an example of how important wisdom, seemingly unrelated, can be used as a guide through an important planning process. For our example, I will use the important choice of insuring one's life to protect our loved ones. Benjamin Franklin once published his 13 Virtues as a reminder to all about aspiring to success. Imagine applying his famous **13 virtues** into the practice of a financial representative taking you through the financial preparation process. It is remarkable to see how these principles are adaptable to our lives and financial responsibilities of today as we move on to the next principle. Consider your financial professionals. Do they share these virtues?

Principle 6

Heed the wisdom of the wise

Benjamin Franklin, Financial Representative?

While everyone seems to have an opinion, wisdom is different. It is the merging of education and experience through learning. Sometimes, wisdom is found in unexpected places. With a bit of poetic license and creativity, let's spread some wisdom by comparing <u>Ben Franklin's 13 Virtues</u> with the stages and issues everyone must address when completing the personal financial preparation process to achieve financial freedom. He seems to have had more insight than we ever imagined. Here's a closer look:

1 Temperance

Or, alertness. Pay attention to your needs and obligations, as well as the professionalism and credibility of those assisting you with planning. There are generally three sources of benefits: The government, an employer or you. None of these sources have the ability or wherewithal to provide you and your family with all the benefits you may need (e.g. disability benefits, life insurance, retirement, etc.). One should not assume that someone else, no matter how well intended, is completely addressing your needs and desires.

2 Silence

Prior to the day that you are silenced forever, all the planning should be done already. Franklin said, "Speak little and do much." Plan your funeral or memorial service. Surprise others by doing more than is expected. In addition to your family, remember your church or synagogue, school, and favorite charity when bequeathing money or suggesting memorial donations after your death.

3 Order

Franklin said, "Let all your things have a place; let each part of your business have its time." Old Ben was telling us the importance of completing important life planning documents: a last will and testament a living will and an ethical will. The planning process must be completed in steps or a defined order. These steps include education, assessments, discussions, and execution.

4 Resolution

An English proverb says, "One of these days means none of these days." Make the commitment to initiate and execute your life insurance plans now. This is a long-term commitment completed by few.

When completed, you will leave a true legacy for your loved ones. According to a study from Penn State University, less than one percent of all term life insurance policies purchased are in force when the insured dies. Most people lapse their policies before they lapse themselves!

5 Frugality

A significant consideration in your life insurance planning process is the disposition of the funds after you die. In other words, what happens to the money? By practicing "capital conservation" (living off the earnings), your beneficiaries are guaranteed a lifetime income. **Do the math.** The amount of life insurance you currently own (or rent) may not produce as much income as you think. For example, a $250,000 death benefit will generate $12,500 a year, if 5% could be earned each year. Before your loved ones can spend it, they must pay taxes, which would leave a monthly income of only about $800 if using a 23% marginal tax rate. Was this less than you thought?

6 Industry

Franklin said, "Be always employed in something useful." We can interpret his meaning to reflect the importance of taking care of your business and important priorities in life. Don't put off until tomorrow what you can do today.

7 Sincerity

Dr. Martin Luther King, Jr. said, "To be honest is to confront the truth. However unpleasant and inconvenient the truth may be, I believe we must expose and face it if we are to achieve a better quality of American life." Discussing death is unpleasant; however, it is a critical discussion that can impact your family for generations.

8 Justice

Dr. King also referred to Franklin's eighth virtue, Justice, in this manner: "Life's most persistent and urgent question is, 'What are you doing for others?'" Leaving a $250,000 life insurance benefit is a good deed; leaving $500,000 is even better. You have the authority and power to guarantee financial freedom for your family for generations. Use this power wisely.

9 Moderation.

Theodore Roosevelt shared profound insurance wisdom by saying, "Keep your eyes on the stars and your feet on the ground." This is an important virtue regarding yourself, more than your life insurance. What are the consequences of owning a lot of life insurance? Can you imagine a survivor saying their dearly departed left them too much life insurance?

10 Cleanliness

As it relates to health. This tenth virtue becomes essential as you prepare to execute your plan. Here is the dichotomy: If you have not taken care of your health, you may be restricted or prevented from purchasing life insurance. It's wise to take advantage of the opportunity to purchase insurance when it is most available at the lowest overall cost. Pay wholesale today or retail years from now.

11 Tranquility

"Don't be disturbed by trifles or at unavoidable or common accidents," Franklin said. The media, so-called experts, and know-it-all peers may attempt to derail your enlightened life insurance planning process as a result of their lack of understanding and virtuous perspective. Focus on these objectives: Maintain the amount of life insurance that you feel will provide more than adequately for your loved ones, and be sure that your life insurance does not expire before you do. This will give you tranquility for the future.

12 Chastity

As it relates to friendship. When you die, almost all of your assets become public through the probate process. On the other hand, your life insurance death benefit is paid to your beneficiaries privately and tax-free and will ensure that your family has confidential funds available. Give your beneficiaries this final act of friendship after you leave them. Proper Trust planning can provide some of the same privacy. Seek legal advice.

13 Humility

A Franklin biographer stated that, "When Franklin first developed his list of virtues, he left out Humility." He finally realized that it's more important to do right than to be right. You may think you are invincible or that death is several decades from now. And you may be right. If not, did you do right by your family? You have more power and control of the outcome than you might realize. Have a conversation with an expert (or two) and reveal all that you can do to make your dreams a reality.

"Well done is better than well said."

B. Franklin

Large Purchase

Are you in the market for a new car? How about a boat or second home? Waiting until the last minute will cost you the most. Is this on your horizon? When will it begin being significant?

Principle 7

Don't do it alone

Get Help!

I would love to have Ben Franklin as a financial representative. While Ben is not available, keep in mind that you don't have to (and shouldn't) do this alone. Seek out expert advice. An investment in a professional financial process provides peace of mind by ensuring your best odds of permanent wealth, comfort and protection. Most accomplishments are not solo projects. In my dedication, I indicated the importance of collaboration with the women in our lives.

Everyone in your life has the potential to be a positive influence. For example, my brother, **Steven Katz**, President of Premier Brokerage Services, Inc. in the Greater Philadelphia area, has served as one of the most important mentors in my professional and personal life. My brother, **Bob Katz**, owner of West Avenue Grille restaurants in Jenkintown, PA has taught me a lot about small business ownership, entrepreneurship and family. My sons, **David Katz** and **Jeremy Katz** also offer thoughts and perspectives of a different generation and feedback only sons can provide. Write a book and you, too, can shout out to your family!

To ensure your best interest is paramount to the plan, be sure a process or systematic approach is utilized in the development of your personal analysis.
This will result in:

- More money for you and your family

- Better preparation and flexibility for life changes

- Increased protection against mistakes and unexpected circumstances

- Peace of mind by ensuring your best odds of permanent wealth and comfort. This planned approach to success is the result of a multi-step process. You must:

    o Set achievable financial and personal goals.
    o Assess your current financial health by examining your habits, assets, liabilities, income, insurance, taxes, investments and inheritance plan.
    o Develop a realistic, comprehensive plan to meet your financial goals by addressing

financial weaknesses building on financial strengths and protecting against the unexpected.
- o Put your plan into action and monitor its progress regularly.
- o Revise your plan to accommodate changing goals, changing personal circumstances, changing financial opportunities and changing market and tax laws.

The planning process requires skill, knowledge, diligence and discipline, but greater rewards make it well worth the time.

Can you identify all of the pieces in your puzzle?

EXERCISE:

Habit Replacement Using a Simulator

1. If you are like most people, you wear your watch on your left hand. This dates back to when a wristwatch was "in the way for right-handed people as they worked.
2. Put your watch on your right hand for the rest of the day. It will probably feel strange.
3. Now, try to wear it on your right hand all the time. Observe how often you place it on your left wrist out of habit.

This is a great exercise. It lets you see how it feels to change an old habit without any real risk since there are no consequences if you are not successful. If you can go two weeks without a slip-up, then take the money out of your change mug and treat yourself to something special. You are ready to use your new skills.

Overcoming Your Arguments Against *Change*

Have you ever heard people argue for their own limitations? Every time people use expressions like "I can't seem to," or "I won't be able to," or "It's difficult for me to," they are really expressing arguments for their own limitations. These phrases and other ones like them represent the opposite of positive and creative thinking. Fear has a way of infiltrating your best judgment. In your personal financial life, fear is frequently expressed in connection with arguing for your limitations. You may not have the same level of competence and, therefore, less confidence. "I am afraid I won't be able to save much money," or "I fear there isn't much money available for savings," or "I'm afraid I've never done that before" are examples of self-defeating statements.

In your job, you learn about strategies, tactics, discipline and more. You become a competent professional, knowing what you need to know in order to face various circumstances that may present themselves to you. When it comes to money, however, you probably have not received the same level of training. Although you may have had a class or two on personal finance in high school or college, it's not likely that it was enough to make you feel that you have the competence or confidence to become financially successful.

This can cause you to feel unnecessarily stressed or worried. Worry is defined as "to feel distressed in the mind, be anxious, troubled, or uneasy." Often, worry is only in your mind and takes up valuable time that could be spent getting closer to your goals. It can even become a habit or way of seeing things. Expecting obstacles can sometimes make them appear. Investing too much mental energy on the negative aspects of anything is worry. *Worry stops immediately when we take action and start doing something positive about the problem.* Competence creates confidence, which defeats fear. Dale Carnegie offers a practical prescription for worry. It's quite simple.

Determine the worst possible outcome and then start doing everything you can to improve it.

Worrying about a troublesome area without thinking creatively about how to improve or resolve it is time wasted. It represents an avoidable loss of time, effort, and mental strength. Instead, think positively and creatively. If your mind can conceive it, chances are pretty good that you can achieve it.

What Are Your "Have To's"?

It now becomes a question of your personal *have to's.* What is it that you *have to do* to reach a certain goal, or attain a desired level of education, or advance in your chosen field, or bring about greater prosperity and financial security?

Some *have to's,* of course, are forced upon us by external circumstances. Most workers *have to* pay Social Security, for example, or *have to* work to earn an income. Many people *have to* care for another person—a child, parent, sibling, spouse, or friend. Illness and injury bring about many new *have to's,* as do career changes and retirement.

Another kind of *have-to* is internal. I *have to* get a good education. I *have to* begin regularly saving a portion of all income received. I *have to* practice my mission daily. People who discover their own *have to's* (the earlier the better) and are doing something positive about them are called motivated. Others who don't know what it is they *have to* do, or those who know what it is they *have to* do and simply do nothing about it, are being manipulated because they take much of their direction from others.

People who spend all of their current income, their future income, and even some of their "if come," end up saving and investing very little. They are also more likely to regularly engage in credit-based spending. People who never seem to make up their minds or take any sort of positive steps to influence their futures ultimately become manipulated. They end up taking their direction from others. We either direct ourselves or are directed and manipulated by others.

What we think about, be it negative or positive, will ultimately come about. What we think about and how we perceive things is the direct result of input. Timely, positive input will result in positive decisions, output, and positive results.

Be very careful about all negative input, especially if it is intended to be humorous or worse yet, if it's sarcastic. The subconscious cannot take a joke. Consider Murphy's Laws, a list of supposedly inescapable laws of life that are meant to be funny but really suggest that we are merely the passive victims of circumstance. A few examples of Murphy's Laws are: "If anything can go wrong, it will," "Nothing is as easy as it looks," "The other line always moves faster," and "The light at the end of the tunnel is only the headlight of an oncoming train." Statements like these make it difficult to stay optimistic because they are positive attitude assailants. It takes practice to avoid them.

"If you change the way you look at things, the things you look at change."

Wayne Dyer

Wealth Transfer

There is no such thing as break-even. You either make a small profit or incur a small loss and consider it – break even. When planning for your retirement and later years, you want to be sure not to outlive your money. You will either run out of money or have wealth to pass along. Hopefully, you will actually desire to leave wealth behind to those you care about, beyond what is needed for Survivor Needs. Are you interested in building your legacy with what is left over and that which you planned for? When will it begin being significant?

Principle 8

Occam's Razor

Occam's Razor

This is a problem-solving principle devised by a Franciscan friar, William of Ockham. He was also a scholastic philosopher. His principle states that *among competing hypotheses that predict equally well, the one with the fewest assumptions should be selected.* In its simplest terms, when there are competing solutions to a problem or competing explanations to a dilemma, then the simplest answer is most often the correct answer. Other, more complicated solutions may ultimately prove to provide better predictions, but—in the absence of differences, the fewer assumptions that are made, the better. With regard to your money attitudes and preparation for financial freedom, you can over-think the best way to approach the challenge. The best way is most likely the most obvious and simplest way. This almost always requires, spending less and saving more; but, you already knew that!

Unlocking Doors in Your Mind

Often we are guilty of putting limits on ourselves by not considering the many possibilities open to us. While we may be aware of much we do not know, the larger threat to our success may come from **what we don't know we don't know.** It may take a moment, but you will get it. Consider the case of Eric Weiss. Weiss was fascinated at a young age with magic and illusion and went on to become known around the world as Harry Houdini. While on a world tour, Houdini accepted a challenge to escape from a jail cell in Wales, U.K. He could enter the cell wearing his street clothes, but he must escape within one hour or he would forfeit a sum of money to the town.

Houdini entered the cell and the door was closed behind him. He immediately took a malleable piece of steel from the lining of his belt. He proceeded to bend and shape it and began picking the cell door lock. When the hour was finished, he had used and reused his flexible piece of steel until there were only little pieces on the floor.

Finally, after becoming physically and mentally exhausted, Houdini collapsed against the cell door—*and it opened.* Why? Because *the door had never been locked in the first place.* Houdini had locked the door in his mind, never even considering the possibility that it might not be locked. This kind of limited thinking is called *stinking thinking.* It invariably leads to negative outcomes and failures.

Avoid Overheated Decisions

Be cautious about making decisions while your mind is overheated by greed, anger, selfishness, or other emotions. The mind does not operate well when it's hot which is why many people sleep on important decisions. Most of the time, the new day will bring a new, fresh perspective. Decisions made in the heat of the moment, however, will often result in negative outcomes.

What we impress in our minds is what we will express in our lives. When we impress our minds with Positive Mental Attitudes (PMAs), we will express them in our living, thinking, and speaking. Developing a positive mental attitude is one way of sending negative thoughts away.

"Happiness is when what you think, what you say, and what you do are in harmony."

Mahatma Gandhi

Evaluating Attitudes and Habits

Prior to making any meaningful changes in our financial lives, we need to know exactly where we are. The first step in this process is taking an assessment. When you interview for a job, the potential employer is assessing your skills, experiences, attitudes, and interests. This enables them to utilize you in a way that will benefit you and the organization best.

With regard to your personal finances, an assessment covers two general areas:

(1) Your attitudes and habits and
(2) A financial summary and inventory

Sometimes this assessment phase is a real eye opener, positively shocking. No matter your reaction, this assessment and evaluation stage will help you identify areas that need change and enable you to devise a fresh, creative plan of action. It will also help you identify your strengths.

On the following pages you will find a self-evaluation exercise with statements about money, spending, saving, investing, insurance, and your financial future. Simply indicate to what degree you agree or disagree with each statement. Remember to measure these statements not only against what you think, but more importantly, what you do in practice. For instance, while most people agree it's a good idea to save money, only three in ten actually save regularly.

This is a self-evaluation. There are no correct answers and no score—only insight. Your responses are for you alone to consider when making attitude adjustments. You are not required to show it to anyone, but are urged to share it with your spouse, family members, and friends.

Above all else in this evaluation exercise, be realistic. The more accurate your responses, the more valuable they will be in determining the precise makeup of your own Wealth-Building Strategy.

"If you don't know where you are going, any road will take you there."

George Harrison

Principle 9

Know where you are

Exercise: Self-Evaluation

Read each statement carefully and then indicate on a scale of 1 to 5 how strongly you agree or disagree. Putting down a 5 would indicate you strongly agree while a 1 would mean you strongly disagree.

- ❏ I find myself spending money impulsively.
- ❏ I'm earning enough money to accomplish my goals.
- ❏ I keep an account of every dollar spent.
- ❏ Setting goals is a necessary step to improving net worth.
- ❏ I know the balance in my checking account to the dollar.
- ❏ I seem to be living from paycheck to paycheck.
- ❏ It's hard for me to say "no" sometimes.
- ❏ Lifestyle decisions are more important than investment ones.
- ❏ I take advantage of coupons, rebates, and two-for-one sales.

"Either write something worth reading or do something worth writing."

Ben Franklin

- ❑ I pay credit card interest that could be going into savings.
- ❑ I am a comparison shopper.
- ❑ I can change my life by changing my attitude.
- ❑ I regularly use credit cards for long-term debt.
- ❑ I expect to be no better off financially than my parents.
- ❑ I often say, "I can't afford it."
- ❑ I am a regular saver, saving a portion of all income received.
- ❑ Saving money has always been a real challenge for me.
- ❑ I live within my income, but don't seem to have much money.
- ❑ I have a spending plan that I follow closely.
- ❑ I'm not afraid of being in debt.
- ❑ I am adequately insured (life, family, home, auto, income, and health).
- ❑ My income doesn't cover my expenses.

- ❏ My spouse and I differ in our approach to finances.

- ❏ I don't overspend on eating out or entertainment.

- ❏ I regularly discuss financial matters with my spouse and family.

- ❏ Other things have come before saving and investing.

- ❏ I expect to increase my standard of living each year.

- ❏ Social Security will not take care of me when I retire.

- ❏ I have a written set of goals and objectives I'm working towards.

- ❏ I have determined my eligibility in my employer's pension plan.

"The circulation of your confidence is better than the circulation of your money.

James Madison

Ask yourself the following questions

1) What does money mean to me?

_____
_____
_____

2) What would I do with a million dollars? Be specific and account for the entire amount.

_____
_____
_____
_____
_____

Now that this self-examination/evaluation has been completed, take the time to review your answers and think about them. You may also want to share your exam with a spouse or friend. Were you generous? Did you *Delay Gratification*?

Healthcare Costs

That which does not kill you costs a lot of money! There are four significant exposures that will most likely contribute to your demise:

Cancer

Accident

Stroke

Heart Attack

Based on your personal health history and that of your family's, which of these do you expect to be your misfortune to experience? When will it begin being significant?

Principle 10

Have a plan

Wealth-Building Strategies

You are now in possession of new information about your attitudes toward money and finances. Albert Einstein said, "Knowledge is the most powerful asset we can possess, but if it is void of imagination and creativity, knowledge has no power at all. Positive productive, creative, thinking is all-powerful."

Changing attitudes and habits begins this way:

1. <u>Discover</u> what and why you want to make a change. Make a <u>decision</u> to bring about the desired changes. A decision is the settling of a question, a judgment, making up your mind, and should reflect firmness of thinking.

2. Next comes <u>determination,</u> the act of setting beforehand, of reaching a conclusion, being settled on a decision or on a fixed direction.

3. This is followed by <u>dedication,</u> a setting apart for a specific purpose, the giving up wholly or earnestly as to some person or end.

"There are those who look at things the way they are, and ask why. I dream of things that never were, and ask why not?"

Robert F. Kennedy

Let's translate these steps of Wealth-Building Strategies:

1. <u>Discover</u> what your financial problems are and why you want to change them.
2. Make the <u>decision</u> to change, using the attitude evaluation exercise as a guide.
3. Be <u>determined</u> to stick with your decision and not change your mind tomorrow.
4. <u>Dedicate</u> yourself to concentrating on the new attitudes and habits you wish to develop. Be patient; it will take about six weeks before it's a habit.

The Greatest Financial Risks

Risk tolerance worksheets are now standard issue with most financial advisors, financial planners, financial representatives, stockbrokers, and investment advisor representatives. They are designed to specifically measure your level of comfort and suitability with certain types of investments, otherwise known as your risk tolerance.

The greatest financial risks, however, are those we have grown accustomed to living with on a day-to-day basis. These familiar risks are listed below. Because of the seemingly slow pace of the accumulating consequences associated with these financial risks, many people indicate in surveys that they sense no serious financial risks whatsoever just because they have become familiar and common and not because they don't exist.

The following is a list of these slow moving financial risks. Ask yourself: Are these risks worth taking in your financial future? Is the problem more costly than the solution?

1. Little or no money going into savings or investments with each paycheck.
2. Living from paycheck to paycheck.
3. Using credit cards to meet and/or keep up with everyday expenses.
4. Not having a spending plan.
5. Unabated poor spending practices and habits.
6. Being uninsured or under-insured (life, health, auto, property, and casualty.)
7. Making minimum payments on credit card debt.
8. Not thinking of others as we pursue our own version of an ideal life and our ability to repair the world.

9. Not verifying yearly earnings or pension and retirement benefits with employers and not verifying your estimated Social Security supplemental pension benefits.
10. Not reviewing your credit files annually or driver's license bi-annually.

Everyday spending decisions, especially credit-based ones, can have a far greater negative effect on savings, and subsequently your entire financial future, than any long-term investment decisions you will ever make.

These decisions include how often we eat out at restaurants, how much we spend on new clothes, furniture, and entertainment, how often we go to the grocery store, whether or not we shop, sales and utilize coupons, and how much we borrow for a new car and how long it takes to pay it off.

Many people routinely waste twenty to thirty percent of their money just through poor spending habits. Most wasteful spending occurs with household and grocery items in addition to most, if not all, credit-based spending decisions. And money poorly spent erodes savings.

A regular saver is someone who saves a portion of *all* income received (*see* **The 80% Solution**). And, a regular saver is someone who saves first and spends what is left over. Becoming a regular saver involves a combination of utilizing better spending techniques as well as developing financial self-discipline. Most people will never become a regular saver if they don't first improve their everyday spending habits and practices. Part of the secret to make this transition is to want it enough to make it happen. After all, people who take the time to plan ahead will have better results and live more enjoyable lives than those that wing it; wouldn't you agree?

Getting Married

You have two daughters? Will your ability to throw the weddings be important to you? In today's world, the groom's family often participates too. Is this an important goal for you? When will it begin being significant?

Principle 11

Baby steps

How do you get into the regular savings habit?

Often the single biggest obstacle is simply getting started. Here are a few tips:

1. Begin saving a dollar a day, or more if you can afford it, and all pocket change. Save every day, including weekends. This should help you put aside an average of $50 a month. It's important to save this way for at least a month, before opening up a savings account, to be sure you get into the habit.

2. Establish a payroll deduction plan for a fixed type of investment or savings plan.

3. Conduct a written review of all income and outgo (money spent), paying special attention to cash purchases. If money isn't regularly going into savings, it's going someplace.

4. Plan grocery trips and use a list. Don't go shopping hungry or with other family members. Keep non-food items off the grocery list and take advantage of coupons and sales.

5. Spend cash. Nothing makes an impression on

your mind like taking cash from your wallet.

6. Ask for cash discounts, especially on major purchases. Take advantage of rebates.

7. Suspend use of credit cards because their message is: *spend money you don't currently have!*

8. Review all of your insurance coverage. This should include life, health, disability home, motor vehicle, household, property and casualty. Make sure you aren't duplicating coverage provided by your employer.

9. Do things for yourself you might pay others for, such as lawn maintenance, washing the car, laundry, painting, etc.

10. Turn a hobby or craft into an income-producing opportunity.

While you may not decide to do all of these things, you can do some or even just one. It took you your entire life to get to where you are today, so you are not expected to solve all of these issues by Tuesday. But, you can at least start the process by Tuesday. Don't you agree? It may take you a few years to be on track.

Remember: **People who plan ahead have better results and more enjoyable lives than those who wing it.** Get the hint? The repetition of these phrases throughout the book is designed to stick and become part of your daily vernacular. You most likely didn't get into this alone and do not have to get to where you want to go alone either. Collaborate.

Here is a simple planning process you can follow to be sure your plan will do what you think it is supposed to do:

DISCUSS what it is that you want in life. Deliberate over what is important to you and that which you wish to accomplish or against which you seek protection.

DISCOVER all that you have done up to this point in your life to actually achieve these financial goals and levels of protection. Look at the numbers and habits. *This is best accomplished in collaboration with a trusted financial professional.*

REVEAL what you still need to do to get to where you want to go. An analysis will uncover the math of your goals and actions. Will your current plan and actual actions accomplish what you have planned? If not, modifications should be seriously considered.

Debt

Usually, you can make more money by reducing your expenses than you can by making more money. Are you strapped, hindered, tied down, stifled by debt? When it gets too bad, it can be an obstacle to achieving any of the other goals and levels of protection. There is a science and art to debt reduction and elimination. While that is beyond the scope of this book, it is also clear that tackling debt intentionally, will make it easier to reduce and eliminate. Is this a factor in your life? When will it begin being significant?

"Setting a goal is not the main thing. It is deciding how you will go about achieving it and staying with that plan."

Tom Landry

Seven Elements of Change

What does it take to change and replace habits? Here are the seven steps that must be addressed. Pay attention to this, it is habit-forming and you will be tested on it later.

1) **Attitude** *"A position assumed for a particular purpose."*

How will you approach all the challenges that are presented to you each day?

2) **Awareness** *"Means having knowledge of something."*

What are you doing today to know more than you did yesterday?

3) **Acceptance** *"Agreeing expressly or by conduct to the act or offer of another."*

Are you willing to accept where you are and what you have to do?

4) **Alternatives** *"Offering or accepting a choice different from the usual."*

Will you consider something new to get something new?

5) **Action** *"The manner or method of performing."*

Do you realize that nothing happens until you do something?

6) **Accomplishment** *"A special skill or ability acquired by training or practice."*

Will you change the way you measure success?

7) **Analysis** *"An examination of a concepts, its elements and their relations."*

Are you willing to **create** and **intentionally succeed**?

Exercise: Attitudes Quiz

I know, you were told there would be no math…

1) My attitude toward my finances should be:
a) serious   b) positive   c) indifferent   d) negative   e) alarmed

2) Attitudes can play a crucial role in my financial success.

 ____True ____False

3) To avoid a feeling of being defeated with my finances, I should:
   a) Discuss it with my family.
   b) Let someone else handle my affairs.
   c) Earn more money.
   d) Develop and implement a spending plan.
   e) Wait and see if I still feel this way in a month.

4) I believe my attitude has:
   a) No influence on others I'm in contact with.
   b) Some slight influence on others with whom I'm in contact.

c) A moderate influence on others with whom I'm in contact.

d) A strong influence on others with whom I'm in contact.

e) A negative effect on others with whom I'm in contact.

5) Changes in attitudes can be motivated by:
   a) Books I read.
   b) People I meet.
   c) Music I listen to.
   d) How I feel inside.
   e) All of the above.

6) Positive thinkers always have more opportunities to choose from than do negative thinkers.
   ____True ____False

7) My spending habits and practices are affected by my attitudes.
   ____True ____False

8) Quick, on the next page, list the seven elements of change (The "A" Team).

1. _____
2. _____
3. _____
4. _____
5. _____
6. _____
7. _____

I told you it would come up again! It's ok to refer back to the previous page. ***Life is an open-book exercise***, unlike the advice your high school teacher gave you. Use all the resources available to accomplish your goals. Call on experts. Do not be reluctant to share the facts surrounding your own economy.

 *Feeling like this?*

"I have learned over the years that when one's mind is made up, this diminishes fear; knowing what must be done does away with fear."

Rosa Parks

Principle 12

Overcome the fear

Retirement Income

Your primary career has ended and now it is time for you to enjoy the many stages of retirement Each of these stages may require different levels of income. This income is derived by the assets you have accumulated through Retirement Preparation and will now be used to generate the necessary income. Do you have plans for retiring strong? When will it begin being significant?

Why won't you ask for help?

Here are some truths about why you may be reluctant to access financial expertise:

1) You are afraid of being found out.
   a) You probably don't make as much money as everyone thinks you do
   b) You probably have more debt than others think you do.
   c) You have not saved as much as you think others have.

2) You are afraid of being sold something
   a) Being talked into something can cause regret.
   b) You don't know enough about the subject and have to rely on others.

3) You are afraid of confirming what you already suspect.
   a) You may have to do something about it now that it's in the open.
   b) Once the bell is rung, you can no longer act or behave like you are not aware of the exposure, issue or consequence.

4) You don't want to fire your current expert.

a) You have been through the process with someone else and may learn that all of their work was not the best.
b) Replacing that person with another professional can be very uncomfortable.

Get over it! If everyone is thinking this, then no one makes as much as you think. Certainly, no one likes to be sold or to find out they have missed something important, and no good work should be undone. Despite all of this, you have to put the interests of you and your family first.

Bring it all home

Conclusion

> **If you don't like what you are getting, change what you are doing!**

Now it is time for you to put all of this into practice. You may have found this book useful as a source of practical information, but nothing happens until you do something. **If you do not like what you are getting in life, change what you are doing.** Only then will you see results.

The suggestions in this book are not magical. In fact, they often are not even original! But if applied with a positive attitude, they will help you achieve financial stability and success. This is all certainly easier said, and written, than done. It has taken you years to form your habits and attitudes, so the gradual modification and replacement of those habits takes time as well. Give yourself a break. Reward yourself along the way as a reminder of why you are changing your behaviors and habits. Once you operate under a premise of abundance, rather than scarcity, the world's opportunities will open up to you. Don't postpone joy or prosperity. Rather, emanate joy and prosperity.

I would not expect that you will adopt all the suggestions illustrated in this book. However, even if you only adopt a few of the Principles you will find yourself in a much more favorable position.

Go forth and learn, read, become disciplined, and prosper. Seek the help of those around you and other professionals. Protect your own freedom - *financial freedom* - and be a beacon for friends and family.

Engage a financial professional to assist you along this journey. Feel free to contact me for a referral in your area. You can either let life happen or make it happen. You get to choose.

Let me know how you are doing on your journey and share your successes or obstacles so I, and others, can learn from where you have been. Write me at rick@rickkatz.com. You have a lot more control than what you assume. Seize it. Create intentional success so your results will be greater than you can imagine. After all, people who plan ahead have better results than those that wing it. Don't you agree?

Disclaimer:

This information is for illustration purposes only. Although great effort has been taken to provide accurate data and explanations, and while the sources are deemed reliable, this information should not be relied upon for preparing tax returns or making specific investment decisions or planning. The information provided in this book is intended to serve as a basis for further discussion with your financial, legal, tax and/or accounting advisors. It is not a substitute for competent advice from these professional advisors.

Having said all of that, what you have read could be helpful in developing your own strategy and plan.

A Final Thought

Don't forget to enjoy yourself on the road to financial freedom. You can't save all of it for when you get *there*. We never know when it will end. Live well and end well. Have a marshmallow. Save two for later. You will be thankful you did!

"Always bear in mind that your own resolution to succeed is more important than any other."

Abraham Lincoln

About the Author

Richard H Katz

Rick has been an insurance and Financial Services professional for over 35 years, holding positions including Financial Planner, Sales & Marketing Consultant, Insurance Company Vice President, Chief Insurance Officer, Chief Marketing Officer and Entrepreneur. Rick has been recognized as a national authority on Family Insurance Planning, Small Business Planning and figuring out how to "Pass the Baton." He has been a Leadership Coach, Community Volunteer and Mentor. Rick grew up in Philadelphia, completing his undergraduate education at the Fox School of Business at Temple University majoring in Insurance & Risk Management and Business Law.

His passion is found in helping families and small business owners experience a glimpse of the future so they can be better prepared for that day-after. Contact Rick at *rick@rickkatz.com* for speaking engagements, coaching, sharing, opportunities or a referral to a financial professional who can help you through this process.

*"Don't cry because it's over.
Smile because it happened."*

Dr. Seuss

INDEX OF QUOTES

John Adams	1
Wayne Dyer	65
Thomas Edison	19
George Eliot	6
Benjamin Franklin	53, 77
Mahatma Gandhi	71
George Harrison	74
Thomas Jefferson	41
Rick Katz	iii, vii, 2, 11, 119
Robert F. Kennedy	85
Tom Landry	95
Abraham Lincoln	112
James Madison	80
Rosa Parks	101
Joan Rivers	26
Dr. Seuss	115
Henry David Thoreau	ix, 34

"People who plan ahead have better results and live more enjoyable lives than those who wing it; wouldn't you agree?."

Rick Katz

Notes

www.ingramcontent.com/pod-product-compliance
Lightning Source LLC
Chambersburg PA
CBHW051539170526
45165CB00002B/802